DESMOND FORRISTAL

COLUM CILLE

The Fox and the Dove

VERITAS

First published 1997 by
Veritas Publications
7–8 Lower Abbey Street
Dublin 1
publications@veritas.ie
www.veritas.ie

This edition published 2013

ISBN 978 1 84730 435 3

10 9 8 7 6 5 4 3 2 1

A catalogue record for this book is available from the British Library.

Cover design by Bill Bolger
Printed in the Republic of Ireland by Gemini International, Dublin

Veritas books are printed on paper made from the wood pulp of managed forests. For every tree felled, at least one tree is planted, thereby renewing natural resources.

CONTENTS

INTRODUCTION

I n the long litany of Irish saints, there are three who are specially honoured. They are Patrick, Brigid and Colum Cille and they have been given the title The Three Patrons of Ireland. Saint Patrick, the man who founded the Christian Church in Ireland, is the principal patron saint of the country. The other two, Brigid and Colum Cille, belonged to a later generation. They continued the work of Patrick in the century following his death, spreading and deepening the faith, giving it the strong roots that have lasted to the present day.

Colum Cille is the least known of the three patrons. Part of the reason for this is his name, which confuses many people. Sometimes he is called Colm or Colum, which is the Irish word for a dove. Sometimes he is called Colmcill or Colum Cille, which means The Dove of the Church. Sometimes he is called Columba, which is the Latin word for a dove. That name Columba gives rise to a further complication. There was another very famous Irish saint and missionary who lived around the same time and was also named after the dove. He is called Columbanus or Columban or sometimes even Columba. It is not surprising that people often confuse him with Colum Cille.

If the average Irish man or woman were asked what they knew about St Colum Cille, they would find it hard to answer.

After a lot of brain-searching they might come up with two facts. The first is that he founded a monastery on the island of Iona. The second is that he started a war by making a copy of another man's book. The first of these facts is true. He did found the monastery of Iona. The second fact is questionable. Some modern scholars have cast doubt on the incident of the book and its copy, one of the most colourful and best-remembered episodes in the whole history of the saints of Ireland.

The problem about most old Irish saints is that we know too little about them. The problem about St Colum Cille is the opposite. We know too much about him. We have more stories told about him, more poems composed by him, more prophecies uttered by him, more miracles worked by him, more visions seen by him, more monasteries founded by him, than by any other of the saints of Ireland. Some of these stories are true. Some of them are false. Historians who have devoted long years of study to the period find it well-nigh impossible to decide which are true and which are not.

There are three main sources for the life of Colum Cille. The earliest and best of these is Adomnán's *Vita Sancti Columbae*, The Life of St Columba, written in Latin about 690. Saint Adomnán was born some thirty years after Colum Cille's death but met many people who knew him. The second is a short life written in Irish by an unknown author about 1160 and known as *The Homily Life*. The third and longest is a compendium of all the traditional stories about Colum Cille which was compiled by Manus O'Donnell, a prince of the O'Donnell family, in his castle in Lifford in 1532. He wrote it in Irish and called it *Betha Colaim Chate*, the Life of Colum Cille. It is colourful, uncritical and hugely readable.

The present work draws on those three lives and on other sources, old and new. Its aim is not to provide a strictly factual account of the life of St Colum Cille but to give the main events of his career, which were described by reliable ancient writers and are accepted by all historians. It includes the best-known tales and legends which have been passed down the centuries, some of them in writing, others by word of mouth. Many of these tales describe events that probably never happened. But this does not deprive them of all value. Folklore is an important source of history.

The Italians have a saying about stories of this kind: *Se non é vero, é ben trovato*, which means, 'Even if it's not true, it's a good invention.' A good invention can tell us a great deal about a historical character, about the way he appeared to his contemporaries, about the way he was remembered centuries after his death. The sheer volume of folklore about Colum Cille shows the impact he made on the consciousness of the Irish people. The man that emerges is a very real and human one: fiery, idealistic, quick to anger and quick to remorse, a devotee of books and learning, a respecter of trees and birds and animals, a lover of his fellow men and women, a fearless preacher of the word and spreader of the kingdom, a missionary who blazed a path for many missionaries, a man who communed with angels and lived his life in the presence of God. Fourteen centuries after his death, he is still a man to be reckoned with.

CHAPTER ONE

THE FOX AND THE DOVE

A ccording to tradition, Colum Cille was born beside Lough Gartan on Thursday, 7 December, in the year 521. Neither the date nor the place are absolutely certain, but they cannot be far from the truth. The day and the month are clearly set down in the old annals. The year is more debatable. Some scholars suggest 520 as a more likely date, others opt for 522. The year 521 is a reasonable compromise.

The place of Colum Cille's birth has also been questioned, but a tradition going back many hundreds of years cannot be lightly set aside. The birthplaces of great men do not forget their claim to glory. It is enough to say that Gartan has always claimed Colum Cille for its own and that no other place has seriously challenged it.

The little jewel-like lake and the rolling Donegal hills that surround it have changed little in fifteen centuries. On the side of one of the hills are the ruins of an ancient church, still held in honour because it marks the place where the saint was born. The event was foretold by signs and portents. Adomnán tells us of the dream that came to Eithne, wife of Feidhlimidh and mother of the future saint.

An angel of the Lord appeared in a dream to the mother of the holy man one night between his conception and his birth. He stood beside her and held out what seemed to be a robe of marvellous beauty, on which the colours of all the flowers were painted. After a short time, he asked to take it back from her hands. Then he raised it and spread it out and released it into the open air. She was sad to have it taken from her and she said to the man of holy appearance, 'Why are you taking this lovely mantle from me so quickly?'

'For this reason,' he said, 'because it is a cloak of such high honour that you can keep it no longer.' At these words, the woman saw the robe gradually moving away from her as if in flight, growing wider than the plains and surpassing in size the mountains and the forests.

Then she heard a voice which said, 'Woman, do not be distressed, because you shall bear a son for the man to whom you are married, a son of such flowering that he shall be counted among the prophets of God. He is destined by God to lead souls beyond number to their heavenly homeland.'

With those words sounding in her ears, the woman awoke.

Immediately after his birth, the new baby was baptised by the priest Cruithneachán. The priest gave him the name Criomhthann, which means fox, but the name did not last. As he grew up, the children he played with began to call him by the more appropriate name of Colum, the dove, and then prophetically expanded it to Colum Cille, the dove of the church. Yet the priest's first instinct was not entirely mistaken. He had evidently spotted a streak of cunning ruthlessness which belonged more to the fox than to the dove and which was to have such sad results in the years to come.

The boy had been sent to live with Cruithneachán as a foster-son, and the good priest soon realised that he had a saint in his care. One night, as he was coming home after reciting the Office in the church, he saw that his house was bathed in light. Going in, he found that the light was concentrated over the face of the sleeping boy. Cruithneachán bowed his head to the ground, recognising that the grace of the Holy Spirit was flowing from heaven upon his foster-son.

The custom of fostering children, so strange to us, was common in Ireland among members of the ruling class. The purpose was to cement bonds of kinship among the different families. Colum Cille himself came from the O'Neill clan, the most powerful of all the clans of Ireland. In addition to ruling the northern part of the country, the O'Neills had for many years held the office of high king, which gave them precedence over all the other kings and rulers of Ireland. Colum Cille was a great-great-grandson of Niall of the Nine Hostages, one of the most powerful of all the ancient high kings. As he grew into manhood, his qualities of wisdom, courage and leadership became more and more evident. People began to whisper that he was surely destined one day to succeed his great ancestor as High King of Ireland. But he himself knew that his true destiny lay somewhere else.

The time came for him to leave his foster-home. An angel appeared to him in a dream and told him to ask God for whatever gifts and virtues he needed. Colum Cille said, 'I choose virginity and wisdom.' The angel answered, 'It was the Holy Spirit that led you to make this excellent choice and, because you made it, God will give you many other gifts. He will give you so great a spirit of prophecy that no-one who went before you and no-one who comes after you will be a better prophet than you.' It was the second time that he been called a prophet by an angel. Colum Cille said a last affectionate farewell to his foster-father, received his blessing, and set out upon his travels.

Student Days

The next few years in his life were spent in a grand tour of the principal monasteries of Ireland. One of the most remarkable aspects of the conversion of the Irish was their enthusiasm for the religious life. St Patrick himself was amazed to see communities of monks and nuns springing up during his own lifetime. 'How is it,' he wrote, 'that the sons and daughters of Irish chieftains are now becoming monks and virgins consecrated to Christ?' Less than a century after Patrick's death, when Colum Cille began his journey, the country was dotted with monasteries. They were centres of learning and holiness, which kept the lamp of civilisation alight while Europe was being overrun by barbarian tribes. In years to come, they were to repay Ireland's debt to Europe by sending great monks and missionaries to the continent, men like Columbanus, Fergal, Gall, and Colum Cille himself.

The Irish monasteries of that time were not the majestic and venerable buildings of later centuries. They were young, makeshift and exciting. Everything was built of wood, the church where the monks worshipped, the refectory where they ate their simple meals, the scriptorium where they copied out the sacred manuscripts, the lecture halls where they studied divine and human wisdom. Surrounding these buildings was a sea of little wooden or wattle huts. Each new arrival at the monastery built his own hut, whether he was an aspirant to the religious life, or a student in search of learning, or, like Colum Cille, a man aware of his talents and anxious to find out how they could best be used in the service of God.

He began with the monastery at Moville, situated on the head of Strangford Lough in County Down. The monastery had been recently founded by St Finian, bishop and abbot and renowned scripture scholar. Finian had spent some years in the monastery nicknamed Candida Casa (White House) in Scotland and may have travelled to the European mainland.

Under Finian's tutelage, the young man deepened his knowledge and love of the sacred scriptures.

As the months passed, the older man began to realise what a truly exceptional pupil he was dealing with. One day when Finian was preparing to celebrate Mass, the acolytes discovered that the supply of wine had run out. Colum Cille went to the well and filled a bucket with water. He blessed the water and it turned into wine. When Finian heard about this, he no longer doubted that the young man was a saint. Colum Cille, on the other hand, insisted the miracle was a proof of Finian's sanctity.

Before he left Moville, Colum Cille was ordained deacon, almost certainly by Finian. Their friendship and respect for one another remained unchanged. Years later, Colum Cille paid a visit to his old master. Finian saw him approaching, with an angel at his side, and he said to some monks nearby, 'Look now and you will see St Columba coming, he who merited to have an angel from heaven as his travelling companion.'

Colum Cille made his way south to another celebrated teacher named Gemman, who lived in the province of Leinster. Under this man's guidance, we are told, he studied 'divine wisdom', which probably means theology and spirituality. Gemman liked to study in the open air, and his pupil sometimes went with him. Adomnán describes a strange incident that happened one day while the two men were reading their books outside the monastery. A girl came running towards them for protection, pursued by a man who caught up with her and stabbed her with a spear. Then he calmly turned to walk away, leaving her dead at their feet. The aged Gemman turned to his companion in horror and said, 'How long, Columba, my good son, how long will God, the just judge, let this crime and our dishonour go unpunished?' Colum Cille responded by passing this judgment on the criminal: 'At the same time that the soul of his victim ascends to heaven, let the soul of her murderer descend to hell.' He had no sooner said this than the evil-doer dropped dead upon the spot. Adomnán tells us that the news of this sudden and drastic retribution spread rapidly and that Colum Cille became famed as a wonder-worker throughout the provinces of Ireland.

His next move seemed almost inevitable. It was only a short journey to the largest and most famous place of learning in the whole country. This was the monastery of Clonard, founded by another Finian, no relation to the founder of Moville. Finian of Clonard has been called the tutor of the saints of Ireland and he is said to have had among his pupils the so-called Twelve Apostles of Ireland, the twelve principal monastic founders of the sixth century. Whether all twelve studied there may be open to question, but there is no doubt that Clonard in the 540s was the most intellectually active and lively place in Ireland, and perhaps in the whole of Europe. The young men who flocked there were the flower of the youth of Ireland, intelligent, enterprising and committed. The ideas they exchanged and the friendships they made were to inspire and support them and to make the second half of the century one of the most glorious periods in the history of the Irish Church and people.

Colm Cille's reputation had gone before him, and he was cordially welcomed by St Finian, who invited him to build his hut next to the church door, probably as a mark of honour. Colum Cille built his hut some distance from the door, which was a sign not of disobedience but of prophecy. Some time later the church had to be enlarged to house the growing number of monks and students, and the new church door was right beside Colum Cille's hut.

Among his fellow-students was an outgoing and energetic young man called Ciarán, son of a travelling handyman, who had brought a cow with him to Clonard to make sure of a supply of fresh milk. The two students became good friends, despite the huge difference in rank between them. An old Life of St Ciarán gives us an interesting glimpse of Finian and his students, who seem to have been as high-spirited and unruly as students of any time or place. It tells how Ciarán came to class one day with his book of St Matthew's Gospel, but before he had time to read the full text for that day's lesson, his neighbour borrowed the book from him. As a result, Ciarán could only answer questions about the first half of the text and the students started a chant of 'Ciarán Half-Matthew' to embarrass him. Finian quickly put a stop to them. 'Not Ciarán Half-Matthew,' he said, 'but Ciarán Half-Ireland, for Ciarán will have one half of Ireland and the rest of us the other.' They were prophetic words, for the monastery Ciarán founded at Clonmacnois was destined to rival in influence the monasteries of Colum Cille.

Two other stories make the same point. One tells how Finian had a dream in which he saw two moons arising from Clonard, one of gold and one of silver. The golden moon moved northward to light up the north of Ireland and the west of Scotland. The silver moon moved eastward to the Shannon and lit up the central part of Ireland. The gold moon was Colum Cille, with the gold of his nobility and wisdom; Ciarán was the silver moon, with the radiance of his virtues and good deeds.

The second story has Colum Cille copying a book, which was always to be one of his favourite occupations. Ciarán offered to copy half the book for him. 'I will repay you for this,' said Colum Cille. 'I promise you that half of the churches of Ireland will take their names from you.'

The two young men moved again in search of further enlightenment. Whether they went separately or together, they both ended up in Glasnevin, which is now a northern suburb of Dublin. A monastic school had recently been started there by St Mobhí, nicknamed Cláiréineach, the flat-faced. Mobhí was a relatively young man himself and a former pupil of Clonard, where he had acquired a formidable reputation for learning and may have been regarded as a more progressive thinker than the venerable Finian. His school in Glasnevin had some fifty students when Colum Cille arrived, and they included two future saints and founders, Canice of Aghaboe and Comgall of Bangor.

Mobhí had just finished building a new church and he asked his pupils how they would like to fill it. 'I would like to fill it with holy men, praising God,' said Ciarán, the leader of men. 'I would fill it with godly books for the use of God's servants,' said the scholarly Canice. 'I would have it filled with illness and disease to bring my body into subjection,' said the ascetic Comgall. 'I would see it filled with gold and silver,' said Colum Cille, the realist, 'not for the sake of wealth, but to set up monasteries and adorn shrines and give to the poor.' Mobhí prophesied that Colum Cille would found a monastery which would be the richest in all of Ireland and Scotland.

Colum Cille formed a friendship with Canice and Comgall which was to last all their lives. In later years they were to be welcome visitors to Iona. It was not so with Ciarán. During their stay in Glasnevin, the two men had a falling out because Ciarán resented Colum Cille's superior social status. We are told that an angel appeared and reminded Ciarán that all he had given up was his father's working clothes, whereas Colum Cille had given up the high kingship of Ireland. This not particularly tactful angelic intervention brought peace between the two, but their friendship was not destined to flourish. Ciarán was to die soon afterwards at the early age of thirty-three, only a few months after founding Clonmacnois and many years before Colum Cille set foot on Iona.

Their stay in Glasnevin was unexpectedly and tragically cut short. A plague which had been sweeping Europe began to make its appearance in Ireland. Mobhí himself became infected with the disease, for which there was no remedy. He closed his school and told his students to return to their homes. He himself died after a short illness.

Colum headed north to his native Donegal. Apparently it was during this journey that he was ordained to the priesthood. The story told by O'Donnell is a strange one. Colum Cille went to Clonfad in Meath to see the saintly Bishop Etchenn and ask for ordination. He was in one of his grandest moods, accompanied by a number of companions who behaved almost like a retinue of courtiers. He had difficulty in finding the bishop, and was rather put out when he discovered that a man ploughing in a nearby field was none other than St Etchenn. His companions told him that it would be beneath his dignity to ask for ordination from a ploughman. Nevertheless, he made his request to the bishop, who refused to answer until he had finished his work. Eventually he unyoked his team, spoke to Colum Cille and agreed to ordain him, but not until the following day.

The ordination took place as promised the next day. After the ceremony, Colum Cille ungraciously rebuked the bishop for having delayed him by a day and told him that as a punishment he would never receive another request for ordination. With that parting shot he continued on his journey.

The whole story contains much that is improbable but may be built on a foundation of truth. It is likely enough that Etchenn of Clonfad ordained Colum Cille and that ordinations at that period were conferred in a rather haphazard manner. It is also likely that Colum Cille was prone to stand upon his dignity from time to time, mindful of the fact that he was of the purest royal blood and quick to remind others of this as well.

He continued on his way until he came to came to the little River Bir that marked the boundary of the O'Neill territory. He blessed the river and prayed that no plague would ever cross it, a prayer which was granted. He was safely home again. His journey was over. His education was completed. It was time for him to begin his life's work.

The First Monastery

Colum Cille decided to found his first monastery in Derry, on the site of the present city. The high king, Aodh mac Ainmhireach, had a residence there and he willingly donated it to the saint, who was, after all, one of the family. The king was somewhat surprised when Colum Cille began by burning the house to the ground and very nearly burning a nearby oakwood as well. He explained that he wished to make a completely fresh start, in a place that would be built from the beginning for the service of God.

The old sources give us little information about how a monastery was founded in those days and where the monks came from. In Colum Cille's case, it is reasonable to suppose that he brought a number of followers with him from Clonard and Glasnevin, fellow students who had come under his influence and were willing to work with him in this new venture. Once the site had been cleared, they could build a rough wooden church and surround it with their individual huts. Natural curiosity would have brought other young men to visit the little settlement, talk to the monks, meet the founder, and fall under the spell of his personality. The huts began to multiply, the community increased, the abbot's fame spread through the countryside, and before long the new monastery was on a sound footing. It became known as The Oak-trees of Colum Cille, Doire Colum Chille, from which the present city of Derry takes its name.

He was probably not much more than twenty-five years of age at this time, but he possessed a natural authority which had nothing to do with his royal connections. He had a growing reputation as a theologian, a scripture scholar and a poet, but it was not his intellectual gifts that attracted people. Rather it was the impression of holiness and wisdom that he radiated, in spite of his youth. It was said that he had a gift of prophecy, that he was able to read minds and souls, that he could see events that were happening far away or in the future. He seemed to live his life in the company of angels and in the presence of God.

Many tales were told about his love for the poor and distressed. He undertook to feed a hundred poor people every day and he kept his word. Unfortunately, the servant in charge of the food distribution took his duties too literally. One day a poor man came for food after a hundred had been fed and he was told he would have to come back tomorrow. He came again the next day and the same thing happened. On the third day he was back once more and once more he was sent away. This time Colum Cille heard what had happened. He rushed after the man, without bothering to put on his cloak or shoes, and caught up with him a short distance away. It was only then that he realised who the man was. 'He fell upon his knees before him,' we are told, 'and spoke to him face to face.' From that day on, there was no restriction on the number to be fed each day.

He could be discriminating in his alms-giving. Two men came to him for money, a gambler and a poor man. He gave a penny to the poor man and a groat, worth four times as much, to the gambler. When some onlookers showed surprise, he told them to follow the two men and see what happened. They found the gambler in a tavern, drinking heartily and sharing his good fortune with others worse off than himself. They found the poor man lying dead upon the road, the penny sewn into his clothes along with other coins he had received. Colum Cille explained that there was no point in giving more than a penny to a man who was soon to die and who only hoarded the money he was given. The gambler, on the other hand, though he was no saint, shared what he had with others who were in need.

Occasionally there was a conflict between his duties as an abbot and his status as a prince. This showed itself in his dealings with the bards. The bards were poets and musicians who wandered the country from one princely house to another, reciting their poems and singing their songs in return for food and lodging. Those who made them welcome were rewarded with flattering verses, those who did not were mercilessly satirised. They did not endear themselves to their patrons by this kind of blackmail, but they had a genuine social function. They were artists in their own way, they were preservers of tradition and culture, and they were the only real outside check on the power of the ruling classes.

Once when Colum Cille was away from his monastery he met a large company of bards who demanded food and gifts. He told them to come to the monastery and he would gave them all they needed. 'We won't go,' they said. 'Unless we get these things straight away, we will mock and revile you.' Praying hard, he brought them to a nearby stream and blessed it. The water turned to wine and he found a number of wine goblets in a nearby barrow or ancient grave. A good time was had by all and the place became known as the Barrow of the Banquet.

The miracle of the water into wine is not very convincing, but the story has importance for the relation between the saint and the bards. As a Christian, he had compassion for their need; as a poet, he respected their art; as a nobleman, he felt it his duty to support them. There may also have been a touch of fear as to what they might say about him if they did not get their way. He was to have more dealings with the bards later on in his career.

The Circuit of Ireland

With the monastery at Derry established and flourishing, Colum Cille decided it was time for him to set off on his travels again. This time he went as a teacher rather than a student, as a master rather than an apprentice. During the next few years he travelled the length and breadth of Ireland, founding monasteries, schools and churches beyond number.

How long he stayed in each place we do not know. When he left Derry, he appointed a priest, a kinsman and trusted friend, to take his place as abbot. We can assume that he followed the same course in other foundations, waiting until they were firmly grounded and then appointing one of the community to take over as abbot before going on to his next project. The success ratio must have varied from place to place, depending on the quality of the abbot and community. Some of them, such as Kells and Durrow, became leading centres of sanctity and learning. Others left little more than a name in the annals of monastic Ireland. Of all his Irish foundations, it was Derry that he held dearest, the place more than any other place that he regarded as home.

The first stop in his journey was at Raphoe, roughly halfway between Derry and his native Gartan. During the building of the monastery, a man working on the mill fell into the millrace and was pulled out apparently dead. Colum Cille knelt beside him and asked God to restore him to life. The man stood up, none the worse for his ordeal. It was in Raphoe too that the ploughman lost the iron blade of the plough. The saint blessed the hands of an unskilled boy, who immediately fashioned a new blade, as perfect as if it had been made by a master blacksmith. Stories like these remind us that the early Irish monastery had to be completely self-sufficient in all things, growing its own grain and grinding it in its own mill. The monastery at Raphoe continued its work of prayer and praise into the Middle Ages, and gave its name to the diocese which now embraces almost the whole of Donegal.

The next foundation was at Durrow, which is near the present town of Tullamore and is not to be confused with Durrow in County Laois. The site was granted to him by the King of Tethba, Aodh mac Brénaind. Over the years the monks of Durrow were to develop a wonderful tradition of art and scholarship and produce two of the masterpieces of Celtic Christianity. One is the sculptured high cross which still stands on the site of the ancient monastery and is adorned with scenes from the Old and New Testaments. The other is the Book of Durrow, a copy of the four Gospels, beautifully illustrated with interlaced decorations and the traditional symbols of Matthew, Mark, Luke and John. A note in the book says it was written by Colum Cille, which is now thought to be untrue. But there can be no doubt that whoever wrote it was inspired by the founder's love of books and reverence for the word of God.

After Durrow came Kells. Diarmaid mac Cearrbheoil, who was at that time High King of Ireland, had a residence in Kells. When Colum Cille arrived at the door in Diarmaid's absence he was not allowed in. As might be expected, he did not suffer this insult in silence. He prophesied that the king's house would henceforth be the dwelling-place of monks and that soldiers would live there no longer.

The high king returned and was told of what had happened. He at once apologised to Colum Cille for the lack of courtesy shown to him and by way of compensation gave him the house and the surrounding land for a monastery. The saint marked out the boundaries and blessed the site and foretold that it would one day be the most distinguished of all his foundations, though his resurrection would not take place there: by which he meant that he would not die and be buried there.

Kells rivalled and even surpassed Durrow as a centre of Celtic piety and culture. The remains of the monastery include a round tower, a number of high crosses in various states of repair and a stone chapel, which is known as 'St Colum's House', though it must have been built long after his death. The greatest treasure that the monastery has left us is the famous Book of Kells. Like the Book of Durrow, it contains the four Gospels in Latin, and it surpasses Durrow in the wealth and beauty and richness of its decorations. Every page, every letter, is an act of homage to the Word of God. It has been called the most beautiful book in the world. It was written about two hundred years after Colum Cille's death but it is still very much his book.

His next foundation was at Clonmore in Meath. He left Oisín mac Ceallaig in charge there before moving on into the territory called Brega, the coastal area north and south of the River Boyne. On the way he paid a visit to the important monastery of St Buite, now known as Monasterboice. The monks did not know the whereabouts of the grave of their revered founder, St Buite, who was said to have died on the very day that Colum Cille was born. To their great joy, Colum Cille discovered the grave and arranged to have the saint's remains enshrined in a manner befitting their dignity.

In Brega he founded two monasteries. The first was on Lambay Island, where he was visited by his friends Canice and Comgall. At their request he celebrated Mass for them in the monastery church. As he began the prayers, Canice thought he saw a column of fire rising above him. He whispered to Comgall, who saw the fire as well. Similar stories were to be told of the saint in other places.

He returned to the mainland for his second monastery in Brega. He chose a site just opposite Lambay, which had a well of plentiful clear water. He blessed a stone cross and donated the essentials for a scriptorium, such as writing tablets and book-satchels, and he presented a book of the Gospels written by himself. He blessed the well, which was called 'sord', an old word meaning 'pure'. Because of this the monastery became known as Sord Colum Chille, from which the present-day village of Swords gets its name.

Colum Cille placed the monastery of Swords under the care of one of his own most trusted monks, Finian the Leper, and entered the land of the Leinstermen. He set up two more monasteries there, one in a place called Druim Monach, whose exact location is not known. The other was in Moone, County Kildare, renowned to this day for the magnificent high cross which still stands on the site of the monastic settlement.

That was the furthest south that Colum Cille reached. He now turned round and headed for his native north by way of the midlands and the west coast. He paid a visit to the thriving young monastery at Clonmacnois, where his friend and fellow-student Ciarán now lay buried. He continued to build churches and found monasteries all along the way. We have the names of some of them, such as Assylin and Drumcliff and Drumcolumb and Tory Island, but few details. There is also an unlikely tale of an attempt he made to found a monastery on Inishmore in the Aran Islands. He was rudely rebuffed by St Enda, who refused to give him any land, fearing that a rival monastery on the island would overshadow his own. Colum Cille departed after warning Enda of all the evils that would befall Inishmore because it had refused to receive him.

Thus came to an end St Colum Cille's circuit of Ireland. How long it lasted we do not know: it must have taken fifteen years or more. Nor do we know how many monasteries he founded, or how many churches he built. There are many places in Ireland which still bear his name, such as Glencolumbkille in County Donegal, though they are not mentioned in the ancient sources. Our information is incomplete. Some of the places he founded were never recorded in writing. On the other hand, it is possible that some of the places credited to him were founded by others, and later claimed him as their founder because of the prestige of his name.

One thing is beyond doubt. Colum Cille's epic journey around Ireland imprinted his name for ever on the consciousness of the Irish people. Like St Patrick and St Brigid, he was becoming a truly national saint, one who touched the lives and hearts and imaginations of people throughout his native land.

Having completed his self-imposed task in Ireland, Colum Cille began to reflect upon his future. According to *The Homily Life*, he remembered a resolution he had made as a youth, a resolution to go on pilgrimage, to leave his native country and preach the faith abroad. He decided that the time had come to keep that resolution, to cross the sea and teach the word of God to Picts and Britons and Saxons.

That is how *The Homily Life* describes his decision to leave Ireland. The *Betha Colaim Chille* of Manus O'Donnell tells a very different story. It is a story of a book and its copy and a great slaughter of men. It is a story which reflects little honour on its hero and for that reason deserves all the more to be believed.

CHAPTER TWO

A BOOK AND ITS COPY

The story begins with Finian and his Psalter. A Psalter was the name given to a book containing the Psalms, the hundred and fifty religious poems which make up the Book of Psalms in the Old Testament. These poems were at the heart of the monastic life. The monks met at regular intervals during the day and night to say or sing the Psalms. This became known as the Divine Office and was, after the Mass, the most important part of the monk's prayer life.

In those days before printing, every book had to be copied out by hand. Each monk needed to have his own Psalter, his own copy of the Psalms, so that he could take part in the Office. This is why the copying of books was such an important part of the life of an early Irish monastery. Some of the copying was done by monks in their own huts. The more elaborate work was done in the scriptorium, where masterpieces like the Book of Kells and the Book of Durrow were produced by especially gifted copyists. They did not confine themselves to the sacred scriptures. Many of the great writings of the ancient world survive only because they were laboriously copied out by Irish monks in the sixth or seventh centuries.

Finian had a Psalter which Colum Cille wanted to copy. This Finian was not one of the two men who were his early teachers, Finian of Moville or Finian of Clonard. This Finian was known as Finian of Dromin, abbot of a minor monastery at Dromin in County Louth. We are not told why Colum Cille particularly wanted to copy his Psalter. It may be that Finian had obtained a copy of St Jerome's translation of the Psalms, which was still scarcely known in Ireland though it was far superior to the older Latin translations then in common use.

Colum Cille was staying in the monastery at the time and he asked Finian for a loan of his Psalter. He did not say that he wished to copy it and he carried out the work secretly and in haste, spinning out his visit until the task was complete. Finally the day set for his departure arrived and Finian sent a youth to bring back the precious manuscript. He found Colum Cille still at his work and the secret was revealed.

There are some improbabilities about this story so far. It is hard to see how someone could spend weeks, perhaps months, in a monastery, engaged in the difficult and delicate process of copying a major manuscript without arousing anyone's suspicion. There were so many things that had to be provided: a suitable table and chair, candles and other lights, inkhorns containing inks of various colours, a selection of quill pens and knives with which to sharpen them, and a supply of animal skins from which the parchment or vellum pages were fashioned. If the story is improbable so far, what follows beggars belief. The compiler of the *Betha* included every old wives' tale, no matter how unlikely. Some of the miracles he quotes are positively grotesque, none more so than the ones which accompany the discovery of Colum Cille's unapproved copying.

The account begins by describing how the youth sent to fetch the book saw a bright light coming from under the door of the church. He looked in through the keyhole and saw that the church was filled with light. Colum Cille was at work on his copy, and the light was provided by the five fingers of his right hand which were blazing like five candles. It is not explained how he could have been writing if his fingers had turned into candles. Even if he wrote with his left hand, it would require another miracle.

It gets worse. When Colum Cille realised he was being spied on, he became angry and he said to the bird, a crane, which he kept as a pet, 'I give you leave, if God gives you leave, to pluck out the eye of that youth that came to spy on me.' The crane obediently put its long thin beak through the keyhole, plucked out the youth's eye and left it on his cheek.

The unfortunate victim ran to Finian and told him what had happened. Finian prayed over him and replaced his eye in its socket, healing him completely. Then he went to confront Colum Cille. The argument between the two men became increasingly heated. Finian accused him of acting unlawfully by copying a book without the owner's consent. Colum Cille denied that there was anything illegal about what he had done. Eventually he suggested that they should bring the case to the highest authority in the land, the High King Diarmaid mac Cearrbheoil. Finian agreed to this. Colum Cille then left the monastery of Dromin. Finian stayed, and with him stayed his Psalter and the copy that Colum Cille had made.

This is the kind of thing that gives miracles a bad name. It would be a mistake, however, to reject the whole story because of the extravagant embellishments which have become attached to it with the passing of time. Irish people felt it was a point of honour that their patron saint should work more fantastic miracles than anyone else's patron saint. Alongside miracles of helping and healing, there had to be miracles of punishment. Anyone who wronged or insulted the saint had to suffer some misfortune as a result, thus proving the power of the offended saint.

All this was taken for granted in earlier times. No-one was expected to take these miracles too seriously. They were intended as a mark of respect to the saint rather than as accurate history. The modern reader should treat these incidents with a healthy scepticism. At the same time, it should be remembered that there is usually an underlying reality, a true story behind the frills. In the present instance, the most likely interpretation is a simple one: that Colum Cille borrowed the Psalter from Finian and brought it to one of his own monasteries, where he copied it at leisure.

The *Betha* goes on to tell of the high king's judgment in a sober and entirely convincing manner. The two men, Finian and Colum Cille, went to Tara, royal seat of the high kings of Ireland. They were brought before Diarmaid mac Cearrbheoil and invited to state their respective cases.

Finian was the first to speak. His case was easily stated. 'Colum Cille has copied my book without my knowledge,' he said, 'and my claim is that the son of my book belongs to me.' It was a simple but strong presentation. The comparison with an animal and its young was an effective one and it appealed to King Diarmaid, who was evidently not a profound thinker.

Colum Cille's case was equally clear but more subtle, perhaps too subtle. 'I contend,' he said, 'that Finian's book has not suffered damage of any kind as a result of the copy I made from it, and that it is not right that the sacred words in that book should be lost or that I or anyone else should be prevented from writing them or reading them or circulating them among the clans. More than that, I contend that I benefited from writing it and that I wished to bring the same benefit to all peoples, while doing no harm to Finian or his book by copying it without permission.'

The high king gave his judgment, perhaps the most famous judgment in Irish history. 'To every cow its calf, to every book its copy,' he said. 'For that reason, Colum Cille, the book you wrote belongs to Finian.'

True to form, Colum Cille, answered with a great cry of defiance. 'You have judged unjustly,' he warned the king, 'and you will pay for it.'

The high king's soundbite has often been acclaimed as the first ever statement of the law of copyright. This is not correct. The modern law of copyright, to put it simply, says that an author has full rights over his writings during his or her lifetime, and that no-one can reproduce them in any form without his or her consent. (After the author's death limited rights are held by his or her heirs for a limited period, normally fifty to seventy years.) In the case of Finian versus Colum Cille, the law did not apply. The original copyright holders, the unknown authors of the various poems that make up the Book of Psalms, were dead for many centuries and their copyright had long ago expired. The only other possible claimant was the writer who had translated the Psalms into Latin and who would hold the copyright in his translation during his lifetime. As we have seen, it is likely enough that the translation found in Finian's book had been made by St Jerome: but he died in 420, more than a hundred years earlier.

The one thing certain is that Finian held no copyright in the contents of his Psalter. This does not mean that Colum Cille was without fault. His behaviour in making the copy without permission, his deceitfulness, his discourtesy to his host, were all reprehensible. But Finian was equally at fault. His unwillingness to let others benefit from his Psalter was selfish and possessive and ultimately indefensible. Though Colum Cille did not attack him directly, he was right in implying that he was depriving people of a source of spiritual benefit. He was right in saying that the judgment was unjust. His own words at the hearing were a far more accurate statement of the meaning of copyright than the high king's simplistic crowd-pleaser.

The two litigants left the royal presence, Finian with his book and its copy, Colum Cille with his deep sense of injustice and his burning desire for vengeance. All he wanted was an opportunity to humiliate the high king as he had been humiliated and to recover the book, which by now had become an obsession. He was fully prepared to use force if necessary, but his own kinsmen were not strong enough to attack the high king. It was at this point that a tragic incident occurred and gave him the opportunity he was looking for.

Among those living in Tara was Curnan, son of Aodh, the King of Connacht. He was partly a foster-son, partly a hostage. His father, the king, could not go to war against the high king. If he did, Curnan would be put to death. It happened one day that Curnan was having a game of hurling with the son of the steward of Tara, one of Diarmaid's most important officials. The game became rough and the two began to quarrel. In the heat of the moment Curnan struck his opponent on the head with his camán and the youth fell down dead. Fearing the worst, Curnán ran to Colum Cille and asked for his protection, which Colum Cille immediately granted.

The protection proved useless. The high king, in a furious rage, ordered his men to seize the boy and make him pay with his life for what he had done. They carried out his orders to the letter, dragged the boy by force from Colum Cille's arms and put him to death.

The high king's fury was fully matched by Colum Cille's. Diarmaid had committed a double crime. He had failed in his duty of hospitality to his foster-son and he had violated the sanctuary which had been granted by the Church. Colum Cille confronted the high king and did not mince his words. 'I will go to my kinsmen,' he threatened, 'the clan of Conall and of Eogan, and I will make war against you to avenge the unjust judgment you gave against me in the matter of the book, and also to avenge the killing of the son of the King of Connacht who was under my protection. I am not content to let God punish you hereafter. I must punish you here and now.' With those chilling words, he left Tara.

The king did not hinder him, perhaps afraid to touch him in public, but he gave orders that none of his subjects should join Colum Cille's forces. At the same time he made private arrangements to have him intercepted on his journey north. His efforts were unsuccessful. Colum Cille spent the night in the monastery at Monasterboice and the following day managed to elude the king's men by taking an unexpected route to the north.

Back in his home country, he had no difficulty in persuading the Kings of Conall and Eogan to avenge the insult done to their leading churchman, who was also their kinsman. In addition, he could now count on the full support of the King of Connacht, who was burning to avenge the killing of his son. The support of Connacht was the factor that could tip the scales decisively in favour of the men of the north.

An Empty Victory
The crucial battle took place at Cooldrevny in County Sligo, a short distance from Colum Cille's monastery of Drumcliff. Colum Cille was looking forward with confidence to a decisive victory. He had every right to feel contented. Thanks to his untiring efforts, thanks to his skill in persuasion, thanks to his achievements over the years and his unique stature in Church and state, a massive army had assembled to do his bidding. He had every right to feel contented but now, on the eve of triumph, he was beginning to feel troubled in his heart and conscience.

The night before the battle, he prayed that his army would win a great victory. Then he saw, or dreamt that he saw, the Archangel Michael, leader of the armies of Heaven against the powers of darkness. Saint Michael reproached him for asking such a favour from God. Victory would indeed be his but he would have no enjoyment from it. He would not be reconciled with God unless he left Ireland and never looked upon its people again.

Battle was joined the following day. Colum Cille knelt in prayer behind his army, his arms outstretched in the attitude known as cross-vigil. On the other side of a little stream, Finian was praying, also in cross-vigil, for the success of the high king's army. It seemed to be as much a battle between the two saints as between the two armies for whom they prayed. As the fighting continued on the field of battle, the high king's men started to fall back, casualties mounting as the men from the north and the west pushed forward irresistibly. Colum Cille watched the slaughter and began to wonder which side he ought to pray for. Seeing the high king in danger of his life, he prayed that he would not be killed and his prayer was granted. Then he sent a message to Finian asking him to cease his prayer. As long as the high king's men saw Finian praying, they would keep on fighting. If he stopped praying, they would lay down their arms and many lives would be saved. Finian recognised the truth of what Colum Cille was saying and ended his prayer. The high king's army laid down their arms. It was a crushing defeat. Three thousand of their men had been killed. On the other side only one man died, having crossed the little stream against orders.

Colum Cille was magnanimous in victory. He left the high king not just with his life but with his crown and his kingdom as well. The famous copy, the cause of all the carnage, was returned to Colum Cille and became the most treasured possession of his own clan, the clan of Conall. The custom grew up of carrying the book around the warriors of the clan before they went into battle, and it was claimed that because of its protection they never suffered a defeat. The book became known as the Cathach, the Battle Book, and it is believed that the old book of the Psalter preserved in the Royal Irish Academy in Dublin is the self-same book that was written by Colum Cille nearly fourteen centuries ago.

Colum Cille himself seems to have lost interest in the book as soon as it was handed over. It had been bought at far too dear a price. That was the consensus among the men whose opinion he valued most, the holy men of the different monasteries and churches, the men who were known collectively as the saints of Ireland. He found himself increasingly under pressure to justify his conduct. An argument which is supposed to have taken place between him and a holy man called Cruimtheir Fraech is very revealing. Cruimtheir began by accusing him of causing the death of many men.

'It was not my fault,' Colum Cille replied, 'but the fault of Diarmaid mac Cearrbheoil for giving a wrong judgment against me.'

'It would be better for a cleric to submit to a wrong judgment than to fight against it,' said Cruimtheir.

'When a man's anger is aroused and he has been grossly humiliated, he cannot submit,' said Colum Cille.

'The right thing to do is to stifle wrath,' Cruimtheir replied, 'before it becomes a cause for remorse.'

'Though a man may do much evil through anger,' said Colum Cille, 'God will still forgive him if he repents.'

'It is better to avoid evil than to seek forgiveness for it,' said Cruimtheir.

'Cruimtheir Fraech,' said Colum Cille, 'do you not know that God and the people of Heaven have more joy in a sinner that comes back repentant than in someone who commits no sin and remains in a state of virtue? We humans have a greater welcome for our loved ones who have been absent for a long time than for those who are always with us. And know this, there is no-one in the world that will reach Heaven more quickly than the sinner who repents. There never has been and never will be a worse deed than the deed of Longinus, and yet it was forgiven because he repented.'

'If that is so,' said Cruimtheir, 'may God make good men of both of us.'

'So may it be,' said Colum Cille.

It is a remarkably sensitive and perceptive picture of a good man struggling with a bad conscience. Longinus was the name given to the soldier who pierced the side of Jesus with a spear and, according to legend, became a Christian and a saint.

On the recommendation of some holy men, Colum Cille went to seek counsel from St Molaise, founder and abbot of the monastery on Devenish Island in Lough Erne. The advice Malaise gave him was the same as he had received from the Archangel Michael on the eve of the battle. 'You must leave Ireland,' he said, 'and never again look upon it, or eat its food or drink its drink, or see its men or its women, or tread upon the soil of Ireland for evermore.'

Still he hesitated. In an effort to resolve the situation, the saints of Ireland held a synod in Teltown, a celebrated meeting place in the territory of the high king. Advice and persuasion had proved useless so they decided on drastic action. They passed a sentence of excommunication on Colum Cille, the severest punishment within their power.

He came to the synod to hear their verdict, a lone and forlorn figure. One of the saints, Brendan of Birr, rose unexpectedly, went to meet him and embraced him with great reverence. The others rebuked him for touching the untouchable but Brendan was unrepentant. 'I saw a pillar of fire and light,' he said, 'going in front of this man of God whom you despise, and holy angels attending him as he crossed the plain. Therefore I cannot despise him, since I can see that God has predestined him to lead the nations on the road to life.'

His words touched the hearts of the assembly. The man they condemned had done more for the Church and the faith and the monastic life than any of those who condemned him. They withdrew their sentence and freed him from excommunication. But for Colum Cille it must have been the most devastating moment of his life, when he found himself publicly condemned and rejected by the men he respected most. He knew now that Ireland no longer had a place for him.

Farewell to Ireland
The battle of Cooldrevny was fought in 561, the first undisputed date we have in the life of Colum Cille. The Synod of Teltown took place the following year, 562. After the synod Colum Cille returned to Derry and began to prepare for exile. He had always loved Derry, but now that he was going it seemed more beautiful than ever. Many poems have survived which are attributed to him but none of them have the same depth of feeling as those that describe his last days among the angel-haunted woods and fields of Derry. They are written in the style of the time, in four-line stanzas which are known as quatrains.

> It is for this that I love Derry:
> For its level fields, for its brightness,
> For its hosts of white angels,
> From one end to the other.

There is not a leaf on the ground
In Derry lovely and faultless
That has not two virgin angels
Facing every leaf.

There is no room on land
For the number of good gentle angels;
Over a distance of nine sea-waves
They reach out from Derry.

The step he was about to take was a pivotal one not only in his own life but in the life of Irish Christianity. A whole new era was beginning. Up to this, the faith was something that the Irish had received from abroad. The precious legacy of St Patrick had been accepted and developed in a uniquely Irish way. Now the time had come for a decisive new initiative. The time had come for the Irish to become missionaries themselves and to bring the faith to the pagan tribes and peoples who had overrun almost the whole of Europe. In the centuries that followed there would be many great Irish missionaries building churches and founding monasteries and leaving their names in the place-names of half a continent. But none of them could claim the glory that belonged to Colum Cille, the glory of being the first Irishman to lead a foreign mission to the lands beyond the sea. The exile that began as a punishment was to be the door to greatness. The prophecy of St Brendan at the synod was to be fulfilled: 'I can see that God has predestined him to lead the nations on the road to life.'

Few details have been preserved about Colum Cille's preparations for his voyage from Derry, but it is not hard to imagine the kind of things that had to be attended to. He decided not to make the journey on his own but to take with him a number of companions who would form a monastic community in whatever place they landed. A boat had to be acquired or built, stout and sea-worthy, since no-one knew what dangers lurked in the northern seas: rocks, storms, whirlpools, icebergs, monsters beyond imagining. Food and clothing would be needed for the monks, enough to feed and dress them until they had found a place to settle. Building and farming implements would be essential to provide housing and furniture for the community and to ensure a steady supply of food. A supply of seed and livestock might also be included, poultry, certainly, and possibly some lambs or calves. The sacred books would have to be brought, together with materials for further writing and copying, vestments for the Eucharist, chalices and other vessels, bread and wine. Then there were all kinds of odds and ends, fishing nets and lines, kitchen pots and pans, tools for carpenters, sheep-shearers, weavers, and a dozen other trades, all part of the daily life of a monastery.

The boat also had to be filled with men. The task of choosing the monks cannot have been an easy one. It is only to be expected that Colum Cille would have chosen his companions from his own monks, most if not all of them from Derry. Wildly different traditions have been passed down about the number who went with him. The *Betha* says that he brought twenty bishops, two score priests, thirty deacons, and two score students that had not yet the rank of priest or deacon, which gives a grand total of a hundred and thirty. A more believable version is given in an old manuscript which says that he was accompanied by twelve companions and gives a list of their names. Three of them were related to him, an uncle and two cousins. The number twelve may have been deliberately selected by Colum Cille in memory of the twelve apostles. It is worth noting that his great successor, St Columbanus, also chose twelve companions when he sailed southward to France some thirty years later.

Winter passed and spring brought finer weather and calmer seas. It was time to go. A great throng of relations and friends gathered in Derry to say a last goodbye to the exiles. Colum Cille was deeply touched by their cries and lamentations. He almost drew back at the last moment. He gave instructions for the boat to leave Derry without him and to pick him up at a place further along the coast of Lough Foyle. He made his way by land and when he arrived there he washed his hands in a stream, from which the place was given the name Glais an Indluidh, the stream of the washing. He blessed a stone that stood nearby and walked sunwise around it and promised that anyone who walked sunwise around it before going a journey would travel and arrive in safety. Then at last he boarded the ship for the start of his voyage into the unknown. It is touchingly described in the *Betha*.

Then they steered the boat through Lough Foyle to the place called Na Tonna Cenanna, The White-faced Waves, where the lake enters into the great sea. And it was not only the people of his country that were sad and sorrowful after Colum Cille, but the birds and the mindless creatures as well. To show their sorrow, the seagulls and birds of Lough Foyle followed the boat on either side, screaming and crying for grief at Colum Cille's departure from Ireland. And he understood their words of sorrow just as he would have understood the words of human beings. So great was his gentleness and his love for his land and his birthplace, that his sadness at parting from the people of Ireland was equalled by his sorrow at parting from the seagulls and the birds of Lough Foyle. And he spoke this quatrain:

The seagulls of Lough Foyle
Go before me and after me,

But they go not with me in my currach;
Ochone, it is a sad parting.

The boat ploughed on through the dark waters and the hills
of Donegal began to fade from view. Colum Cille kept his
eyes on them while land and sea and sky began to merge into
one. Then he spoke his last Irish poem.

I stretch my eye across the brine
From the firm oaken planks;
Many the tears of my soft grey eye
As I look back upon Ireland.

There is a grey eye
That will look back upon Ireland;
Never again will it see
The men of Ireland or its women.

At dawn and at eve I lament;
Alas for the journey I go!
This is my name – I tell a secret –
'Cul re hErind'.

The secret name of Colum Cille, Cul re hErind, sums up in
three heart-breaking words all the mixture of emotions that
were surging within him. It means 'I turn my back upon
Ireland'.

CHAPTER THREE

THE ISLAND SOLDIER

In the second year following the battle of Cooldrevny, at the age of forty-two, Columba sailed from Ireland to Britain, desiring to be a pilgrim for Christ.

From boyhood he had devoted himself to the Christian discipline and to the study of wisdom; he had through the grace of God kept his body chaste and his mind pure; and he had shown himself, while still on earth, fit to be a citizen of Heaven. Angelic in appearance, refined in speech, holy in action, outstanding in intellect, gifted in counsel, for thirty-four years he led the life of an island soldier.

He could not let so much as an hour pass by without giving himself to praying or reading or writing or some other form of work. Day and night, tirelessly and without pause, he devoted himself to fasts and vigils, any one of which might seem beyond human endurance. And with all this, he remained loving towards everyone, his face cheerful and holy, his heart filled with the joy of the Holy Spirit.

Those words are taken from the preface which St Adomnán wrote for his most celebrated book, *The Life of St Columba*. Adomnán, sometimes known as

Eunan, must be our main source of information for the remainder of our story. The old Irish Lives tell us little about the second half of Colum Cille's life, the years he spent in Scotland, exiled from his native land. Adomnán fills in the gap.

The Colum Cille whom Adomnán presents is a different man from the Colum Cille of the Irish Lives, gentler and kinder and more appealing. To some extent this may be because Adomnán wanted to show the founder of his monastery in a good light and to pass over anything that would be to his discredit. But there is more to it than that. The evidence strongly suggests that Colum Cille underwent a deep change, which might almost be called a conversion, in those two years between the battle of Cooldrevny and the leaving of Ireland.

Before Cooldrevny, he had already proved himself to be a man of outstanding achievement and force of character. Other saints of the time were content to found one monastery and nurture it into full maturity. Colum Cille founded a whole network of monasteries and churches without parallel in Irish history. He used all his natural gifts to the full, his power of leadership, his organising ability, his perseverance, his courage in the face of obstacles. He also made use of his noble birth, which enabled him to speak to kings as an equal and to command the obedience of lesser mortals.

All these qualities, useful though they were, had a reverse side. Leadership can easily become dictatorship. He did not suffer fools gladly. He had little time for the objections of others and little care for their feelings. People who crossed him in any way, people like Etchenn and Finian and Enda and Diarmaid, felt the full power of his wrath. He was unduly conscious of his birthright as a member of the ruling class. He withstood kings to their face and made commoners acutely aware of their inferiority.

Such is the picture of the man that emerges from the old Irish Lives and traditions. The greatness of the man is not questioned. His prayerfulness, his dedication, his extraordinary powers, natural and supernatural, are constantly brought before us. But it is a picture that has darkness as well as light. Individual stories about this dark side can be challenged but not their general effect. They faithfully reflect the impression that Colum Cille left upon the folk memory of the Irish people. He was a great man but a hard man too.

The two years between the battle and the exile were his time of purification. Three thousand men had died because of his obstinacy, and all his great powers could not bring them back to life. One tradition says that he was ordered to atone for the lives he had lost by winning the souls of three thousand pagans for Christ. If that is true, he made atonement many times over during the remaining thirty-four years of his life.

The monks' voyage took them along the western coast of Scotland, passing the mainland peninsulas and the scattered islands of the Inner Hebrides. They finally made their landfall on the small and remote island of Iona, separated by a narrow strip of water from the larger island of Mull. It is not known why they chose this island. It may have been that it was uninhabited and there was no-one to object to their arrival. It may have been that they now felt they were sufficiently far from home. One touching old legend says that Colum Cille stopped at every island on the way until he found one from which he could no longer see Ireland. He climbed the modest hill which was the highest point on Iona and looked back in the direction from which he had come. No hill or mountain-top broke the long level line of the horizon. His exile was complete.

Western Scotland was not completely uninhabited at that time. Over the years a number of Irish colonists had founded small settlements along the indented coastland. Most of these people belonged to the Dal Riada, a tribe living in the Antrim area, the part of Ireland that is nearest to Scotland. When they crossed the sea they retained the name of Dal Riada. The majority of them were probably Christians and they are likely to have brought some priests and monks with them. At first they owed a vague allegiance to the High King of Ireland, but with the passing of the years they became more independent. By the time of Colum Cille's arrival they obeyed only their own local king, Conall mac Comgaill, and resented any attempts of the high king to assert his authority.

Eastern Scotland was the home of a very different people, the Picts. They got their name from their custom of painting their bodies when going into battle. The Romans called them *picti*, which means 'painted men'. Scarcely anything is known about them, their origins, their way of life. They left little in the way of art, still less in the way of literature. They had their own language and customs and religion. They had not accepted Christianity, and may never have heard of it. They were known and feared for their ferocity in battle and had prevented the march of the powerful Roman army into Scotland. They had no love for the Irish settlers and would have swept them into the sea if there had not been a huge mass of mountains separating their two territories.

Colum Cille and his monks landed on Iona on 9 June 563. Their first task was to build themselves a home. The long northern summer days meant that they could work for hours building their church and their huts, and laying out fields and farmyard. It was late in the year for planting and they must have depended on others for food and other necessities during their first autumn and winter. No doubt they were helped by the people of the Dal Riada, their fellow-countrymen. It is hardly necessary to add that the King of Dal Riada, Conall mac Comgaill, was a close relation of Colum Cille.

A plan of campaign soon presented itself, indeed forced itself upon the saint and his community. The first step was to establish their monastery and provide all that was needed for their daily life of prayer and work. The second step was to reach out to others, providing spiritual leadership and support to the Christians of the Dal Riada. As the number of monks grew, they would build churches and even monasteries on the islands and mainland of the Irish settlement. The third and most decisive step would be to turn to the pagans, to cross the physical and spiritual divide, to bring the gospel message to the fearsome Pictish people and to win them for Christ. The fourth step, a long way down the road, would be to evangelise the people of England, where Christianity had been almost completely extinguished by the invasion of the barbarians. And so it happened, though the final step, the conversion of northern England, took place after Colum Cille's death through his spiritual child St Aidan, one of the greatest of the monks of Iona.

Prophecies, Miracles, Apparitions

Saint Adomnán's biography provides us with a wealth of information about the development of Iona but it does so in a manner which seems strange to the modern reader. Instead of beginning at the beginning and going on to the end, Adomnán divides his work into three books, each dealing with a different aspect of Colum Cille's personality. He describes the three books as follows: 'The first of these contains prophetic revelations; the second contains divine miracles worked by him; the third contains apparitions of angels and appearances of heavenly light above the man of God.'

He goes on to describe his working method. 'Let no-one think that anything I write about this remarkable man is untruthful or doubtful or uncertain. I write only of the traditions handed down by trustworthy and well-informed elders and I recount them without ambiguity, whether I diligently discovered them in written accounts or heard them from the lips of trustworthy and knowledgeable old men, who spoke with absolute certainty.' This is the method of a true historian, tracking down verbal and written accounts, accepting those which are well vouched for, rejecting those which belong to the world of religious fantasy. There, is a world of difference between his patient scholarship and the *Betha's* uncritical acceptance of every tale and legend, no matter how improbable.

Adomnán in theory restricts himself to his three categories of prophecies, miracles and apparitions. In practice, he cannot help giving us a vivid and lifelike picture of the life of the community on Iona, a life which he shared in for so many years, and an even more lifelike portrait of its great founder and abbot, St Colum Cille. The little story of the man and the inkhorn is a typical example of his style.

> One day a shout was heard from the other side of the Sound of Iona. The saint was sitting in the hut raised on wooden beams and he heard the shout and said, 'The man who is shouting across the Sound is a clumsy kind of person and today he is going to knock over my inkhorn and spill it.' Hearing this, his servant Diarmaid took up his stand beside the doorway, to await the arrival of the troublesome visitor and protect the inkhorn. But after a while he left for some reason, and after he had gone the unwelcome visitor arrived. When he went to embrace the saint, the edge of his cloak struck against the inkhorn and spilt it.

It is a simple little story but it brings the setting to life for us. We see a monastery and an abbot who were open to anyone who came to visit them. All the visitor needed to do was to stand on the edge of the Sound, the stretch of water between the island and the mainland, and shout. A boat would put out from the island and take him across to the monastery. The abbot had his own little hut, raised on wooden beams to protect it from dampness, and here he spent much of his time writing and copying.

The story is included among the prophecies, because Colum Cille foretold the spilling of his ink. It is a homely kind of prophecy, as are many of the prophecies related by Adomnán. Colum Cille was not so much a prophet as a man endowed with a sixth sense, a man with a supernatural sensitivity towards people and events. He was particularly sensitive towards danger and death. He was aware of friends in difficulty, in sickness, in battles on land, in storms at sea. He would know when someone he loved died and he would pray for his or her soul. Most people have extra-sensory experiences from time to time; with Colum Cille they were an almost daily occurrence.

Another little prophecy underlines the importance of books and copying in the work of the monastery.

> Baithéne came to him one day and said, 'I have copied out the Psalter and I need one of the brothers to go over it with me and make corrections.' Hearing this, the saint said, 'Why put this unnecessary burden upon us? In this Psalter that you are talking about there is not a letter too many nor a letter too few, except for one letter "I" which is missing.' They went through the whole Psalter and found it was exactly as the saint had foretold.

Open to the World
The saint's hut was no ivory tower. It was open to the world. Important people came to see him, kings, bishops and saints, asking for his advice and his prayers. He was equally available

to the poor and the unimportant. The young dairyman would stop outside the door each day on his way from milking the cows and hold up the bucket of milk for the saint's blessing. On one occasion a specially powerful blessing was needed. A devil had hidden himself in the pail because the dairyman had forgotten to make the sign of the cross over it. It took all Colum Cille's strength to drive out the enemy and restore the milk to its natural goodness.

Ordinary people came to him with their troubles. He would put down his pen, listen to their woes and give them his advice and his blessing. Marriage counselling was among his skills. A couple came to him, the husband complaining that his wife no longer loved him. She admitted this, saying that she would do anything the saint asked, even enter a convent, as long as she did not have to share her husband's bed. The saint prayed and fasted with them that day and sent them home for the night. Next day he asked the woman if she was prepared to enter the convent. She answered, 'Now I know that God has heard your prayers for me. The man I hated yesterday, I love today. Last night, I do not know how, my heart was changed from hatred to love.' Adomnán numbered this among the miracles that showed Colum Cille's sanctity. Others might wonder if he shrewdly judged that when the woman was forced to choose, she would prefer the husband to the convent. In any event, Adomnán assures us that the couple lived happily ever after.

There is a touch of the fairy-tale about many of the stories. One of the quaintest concerns a poor man who came to Colum Cille and asked for food for his wife and children. The saint was always generous with alms for the needy, but this time he offered something quite unique. He took a wooden stake, sharpened the point and gave it to the man, saying, 'As long as you have this stake, your household will never be short of venison to eat.'

The man went home and stuck the stake in the ground in a nearby forest. Next morning he found a large stag impaled on the stake, food for many days. As time went on, the stake continued to provide animals for himself and his family and he even had enough to sell meat to his neighbours.

But then the devil began to work on his wife and she began to work on her husband. 'Take up that stake from the ground,' she told him. 'If any person or farm animal is killed on it, you and I and our children will be put to death or sold into slavery.' Eventually he gave in to her pressure, uprooted the stake and brought it back to his house. Shortly afterwards, one of the house-dogs fell on it and was killed. The wife returned to the attack. 'One of the children is going to fall on the stake and be killed,' she said.

The man brought the stake back to the woods and set it up in a place so overgrown that no animal could reach it. The next day he went back and found that a goat had fallen on it and been killed. Then he pushed the stake into the river bed beneath the surface of the water; he came back and found a huge salmon impaled on it. He took the stake again and this time placed it on the roof of his house, well out of harm's way; but a passing raven fell upon it and was killed. It was too much. Spurred on by his wife, the man chopped the stake into little pieces and threw it on the fire. He and his family returned to their poverty and they bitterly regretted the loss of the stake that had been their constant provider.

Apart from the fact that they did not live happily ever after, this has all the air of a fairy-tale, and a comic one at that. It is a delightful story but is hardly meant to be taken seriously. It is not impossible that it was palmed off as a joke upon the unsuspecting Adomnán. He was a good man and a diligent scholar but he may not have known when his leg was being gently pulled.

A more convincing picture of Colum Cille is found in those stories which show his love for birds and beasts, a characteristic found in almost all the Celtic saints. Typical of these is the story of the lost bird.

> On another occasion, when the saint was living on the island of Iona, he called one of the brothers and said, 'On the third day from this morning, you will wait on the western side of the island, sitting on the seashore, because a guest will arrive from the northern region of Ireland, a crane buffeted by long exposure to the winds. It will fall on the shore in front of you and lie there, drained of all its strength. You will be careful to lift it up gently and take it to the house nearby. There you will make it welcome and nurse it for three days and nights and feed it caringly. It will recover after the third day and, no longer wishing to remain in exile with us, it will return to its former home, the sweet region of its native Ireland, fully restored to health. I ask you to do all this carefully, because the place it comes from is my own native place.'

Adomnán includes this story among the saint's prophecies and tells us that everything took place exactly as he had foretold.

As the years passed, Colum Cille's influence grew and deepened throughout the territory of the Dal Riada. The number of visitors to Iona increased steadily, some to seek advice and help, others to join the monastic community and dedicate their lives to God. No-one was turned away from the door of his little hut, though the stream of visitors left him little time for work or prayer. His reputation as a seer and a wonder-worker made him uncomfortable and he asked the brothers not to spread stories about him which would attract still more visitors.

As the number of monks increased, the saint was able to found churches and monasteries on the islands and mainland. Little is known about them and even the names of most of them are forgotten, but they played an important part in building up the faith throughout the Dal Riada. The ones most often mentioned by Adomnán are the monasteries on the islands of Tiree and Hinba. The Tiree monastery was near enough to Iona and Colum Cille often stayed there. He was also a frequent visitor to Hinba, whose precise location is no longer known. There is no place of that name today and scholars are unable to agree which of the Hebridean islands was once called Hinba.

People who wished to retire for a time from the world and do penance for their sins could stay in one of the island monasteries. One of these was Fiachnae, a man of great wisdom and learning, whose coming was foretold by the saint. When he arrived, he threw himself weeping at the saint's feet and confessed his sins in front of everyone. Colum Cille comforted him: 'Arise, my son, and be consoled; the sins you have committed are forgiven. As scripture says, the Lord will not despise a contrite and humble heart.' He sent Fiachnae to find peace of soul in Tiree.

He dealt differently with two brothers who came to Iona and asked if they could spend a year as pilgrims in the monastery. Colum Cille embraced them and then answered, 'Your request to spend a year of pilgrimage with me cannot be granted unless you first take monastic vows.' This surprised the brothers and everyone else, because candidates had to undergo a period of probation before being allowed to take their vows. The older brother said, 'Although we had not intended this, we will do what you say, because we believe your words are inspired by God.' The saint led them to the church, where they knelt and devoutly pronounced their vows. Then the saint turned to the members of the community and said,

'These two candidates are offering themselves as a living sacrifice to God and fulfilling years of Christian service in a short time, for within a month they will pass in peace to Christ the Lord.' Soon after this, both of them fell ill and they had gone happily to their God before the end of the month.

There was a less happy outcome in the case of a man who arrived from Ireland and swore he would eat no food until he had met and spoken to Colum Cille. For once, the saint was unwilling to meet a penitent. 'This man,' he said, 'has killed his brother as Cain did, and has seduced his own mother.' Nevertheless he saw the man, who promised to fulfil any penance that was laid upon him. The saint told him he must spend twelve years repenting his sins in a Welsh monastery and never return to Ireland. Then he said sadly to his monks, 'This man is a son of perdition. He will not fulfil his penance as he promised. He will soon go back to Ireland and in a short time he will be slain by his enemies.' It all happened exactly as the saint had prophesied.

The Assembly of Druim Ceat

The King of Dal Riada, Conall mac Comgaill, died in 574. What happened next showed the extent of Colum Cille's influence among the nobility and people of the kingdom. In the Irish tradition, a king was succeeded not by his eldest son but by whichever member of his extended family was considered most fit to wear the crown. In theory this should have been a means of ensuring good kings and good government. In practice it led to all kinds of intrigues and conspiracies which often ended in pitched battles.

There were two leading candidates for the kingship, two brothers who were cousins of the late king, Aedán mac Gabráin and Éogenán mac Gabráin. It was left to Colum Cille to decide which of them should rule the people of Dal Riada. He was staying at the time in the monastery on Hinba and one night an angel appeared to him carrying a glass book called *The Book of the Ordination of Kings*. The saint opened the book and read that he was to ordain Aedán king; this he flatly refused to do, because he was convinced that Éogenán was the better man. The angel struck him on the side with a whip, whose scar remained for the rest of his life. For three successive nights, the angel appeared in the same way with the same book and gave the same command. Colum Cille resisted no longer. He left Hinba and returned to Iona, where Aedán also arrived, hoping for the saint's blessing. The arrangements were quickly made and the inauguration took place there and then upon the island of Iona. During the course of the ceremony, the saint foretold the future of Aedán's line, his children and his grandchildren and his great-grandchildren. Then he laid his hands upon his head, consecrated him and blessed him. It was the first ever Christian coronation of an Irish king.

Aedán proved to be a strong and capable ruler but no saint. Like many of the people of Dal Riada, he seems to have kept traces of the old pagan traditions beneath his Christian veneer. He was happier on the battlefield than in the church and preferred hammering Picts to beating his breast. In his relations with Colum Cille he was respectful but often baffled. One incident recorded in the *Betha* is revealing, if not necessarily true.

It began when Colum Cille sent Baithéne, his right-hand man, to conduct some business with the king. Aedán used the opportunity to question Baithéne about the saint and particularly about his unbroken vow of virginity, which he found difficult to believe. Shortly afterwards, when Colum Cille was on a visit to the king, he decided to put him to the test. He brought in his daughter, dressed in her finest robes, and put her sitting near the saint. Then he began his interrogation.

'She is a beautiful girl,' he said.

'She is indeed,' said Colum Cille.

'Would you like to lie with her?' asked the king.

'Yes, I would,' said Colum Cille.

This was not what the king expected. 'Listen,' he said, 'listen to the man who is said never to have lost his virginity, and now he is saying he would like to lie with this girl.'

'I can't tell a lie,' the saint answered. 'You must know, Aedán, that there is not a person in the world who doesn't have the desire to sin. But whoever turns away from that desire will be crowned in the Kingdom of God. And be sure of this, that I wouldn't lie with the maiden for all the lordship of the world, even though I have the desire to do so because of my lustful human body.'

It is interesting that this conversation is found in the *Betha* but not in Adomnán. It is the kind of incident which Adomnán would prefer to omit, because it might show the saint in a somewhat earthy light. But the candid realism is refreshing and shows a human side of Colum Cille that is distinctly appealing.

It was not long before Aedán had to seek the saint's advice on a different and much weightier matter. Relations between the Irish in Scotland and their cousins in the home country were becoming increasingly strained. The Scots Irish were finding it hard to keep their independence in the face of increasing demands from the Irish Irish. The High King of Ireland, Aodh mac Ainmhireach, was claiming to be the overlord of the Scottish Dal Riada. He insisted that they must admit his sovereignty and pay him taxes and services. The Irish in Scotland insisted that they would do no such thing. No compromise seemed possible and there was a strong likelihood that the dispute would sooner or later end in war. There was only one man who could act as mediator, only one man who was equally respected in Ireland and in Scotland. That man was Colum Cille.

It was not an easy decision for Colum Cille to make. Twelve years ago he had left Ireland, vowing that he would never return. How could he break this vow and return to his native country? But how could he refuse if his coming meant the difference between war and peace? He had left Ireland in atonement for those killed in a battle which he had provoked. To remain in Iona would make nonsense of his vow, because by staying there he could be responsible for another battle and the loss of many more lives. The truly Christian thing for him to do was to swallow his pride, accept the office of mediator and visit his homeland once again.

The meeting between the two kings was held in a place called Druim Ceat, not far from Derry. The principal item on the agenda was the settlement of the dispute between Aodh mac Ainmhireach, High King of Ireland, and Aedán mac Gabráin, King of the Scottish Dal Riada. Two other items were added by Colum Cille himself. One was the ill-treatment by the high king of one of his hostages, and the other was the threat to the liberty and independence of the poets and bards of Ireland.

One old poem gives a highly coloured description of the assembly of Druim Ceat and of the distinguished participants.

> Fifty saints around Colum there,
> Around the two Ciaráns and Comgall,
> Mobhí, Canice, sweet Laserian,
> The two Finians and the two Brendans.
>
> All those, in truth no poor gathering,
> At the Assembly of Druim Ceat,
> Making the peace, a noble cause,
> Between Aodh and Aedán.

The fact that several of the saints listed were long since dead does not take away from the solemnity of the picture. This is poetry, not history. The same can be said about another poem, which tells how Colum Cille arrived with a retinue of forty priests, twenty bishops, fifty deacons and thirty students. In all likelihood, he did have a substantial retinue. It was important that he should present an impressive appearance as a man of royal blood, a man on whom the success or failure of the whole meeting would depend.

It must have been an emotional time for the saint when he found himself back in the beloved country which he thought he would never see again. He may have recalled the sentence pronounced on him by St Molaise on Devenish Island during those terrible days after the battle of Cooldrevny. 'You must leave Ireland, and never again look upon it, or eat its food or drink its drink, or see its men or its women, or tread upon the soil of Ireland for evermore.' Some later writers, recalling these words, spread the story that when the saint came to Ireland he obeyed Molaise to the letter: he wore a blindfold over his eyes so that he would not see Ireland or its people; he lived on supplies he brought with him from Scotland so that he would not eat Irish food or drink; he tied a sod of Scottish earth to the sole of each foot so that he would never again tread upon Irish soil. The story is memorable but not believable. There was no need for him to engage in such pantomime antics. He was visiting Ireland as a foreigner with a short-term visa. When his task was over he would go back at once to the Scottish island that was now and for ever his home.

His first aim was to do what he could for the high king's hostage, Scannlan, son of the King of Ossory. The high king had guaranteed to Colum Cille that he would release Scannlan after a year and take another hostage in his place. He broke his word. The saint found the unfortunate young man loaded with irons in a little wattle hut, with nothing to eat except salted meat and only the most meagre ration of water to quench his thirst. Colum Cille blessed him and told him not to lose heart. He would be released and, after a short exile, he would return to Ossory and reign over it as king for thirty years. All this took place as the saint had prophesied.

The next item on his agenda was the status of the bards. It was a perennial problem in Gaelic Ireland. It was easy to make a case against them. They roamed the country, often in large and unruly groups, demanding food and lodging. They rewarded their patrons with songs of praise, but those who were deemed insufficiently generous were mercilessly satirised. The Irish princes were surprisingly thin-skinned when exposed to the mockery of the bards. An enemy that attacked them with sword and spear could be met with the same weapons. But they had no protection against an enemy who attacked with the blistering bitterness of words. They would gladly see the bards deprived of their privileges and reduced to a respectful silence.

Colum Cille, as a member of a princely family, could sympathise with this attitude. As a poet, however, he had a fellow feeling for the bards and an understanding of the contribution that their poems made to Irish life. The eulogies they composed for their princes preserved the history of the different kingdoms and territories. The brutal satires had their value as a check on the power of the ruling class, and a defence of the poor and oppressed. More than a thousand years later, the great satirist Alexander Pope made the same discovery.

> Yes, I am proud: I must be proud to see
> Men not afraid of God, afraid of me:
> Safe from the bar, the pulpit and the throne,
> Yet touched and shamed by ridicule alone.

This was not, needless to say, the argument that Colum Cille used with the high king, who had made up his mind to outlaw all the bards and drive them from the country. 'This is my judgment, that the poets should be kept in Ireland,' Colum Cille told him.

'It is not easy to keep them, for they are so many,' said the king, 'and it is hard to satisfy them, for they make so many unjust demands.'

'Do not say that,' answered Colum Cille, 'for the praises they compose for you will be as long-lasting as the praises they made for Cormac mac Airt, son of Conn. The praises will endure long after the treasures and riches given for them have perished.'

The comparison with the great King Cormac was enough to convince the king that a bard was good value for money. He agreed to let the bards remain under the conditions recommended by Colum Cille. These were that the bards should not roam the country but should remain in the service of the ruler of their own territory, and that their main function should be to compose poems in praise of him and his ancestors.

And so it was that the poets of Ireland were reprieved and allowed to carry on their trade. Their right to travel was restricted and their right to compose satires left unclear. However, Colum Cille can have had little doubt that satires would reappear before very long. The main point had been won. Ireland was and would remain a country where the poet and his craft were treated with all due reverence.

There remained only the question of the relationship between the King of Dal Riada and the High King of Ireland. Colum Cille appointed a young disciple of his, Colman mac Coimgallain, to deliver his judgment. The actual terms of the settlement are unclear, but the important thing is that it was accepted by both parties. It appears that the King of Dal

Riada acknowledged the status of the high king but had only to offer him nominal tributes and services. The result was that King Aedán mac Gabráin now had a free hand to rule his kingdom and expand it to the best of his ability without reference to any overlord. Aedán was to rule for another thirty years or more and during that period he was engaged in more or less continuous warfare against the Picts and other tribes in Scotland. Some of his battles he won, others he lost, but the final result was to set his kingdom on a firm footing, with the holy island of Iona as its spiritual centre.

His mission in Ireland accomplished, Colum Cille returned to his monastery. He too was planning the conquest of the Picts, but it was a spiritual conquest that he had in mind.

CHAPTER FOUR

COLUM CILLE IN PICTLAND

The Irish in Scotland lived in the western coastal region, separated by a few miles of sea from their homeland in Ireland. The Picts lived in splendid isolation along the cold northern and eastern coasts, with three hundred miles of wild North Sea between them and Norway, the nearest land. The two races were sworn enemies, each constantly trying to extend its territory at the expense of the other. Skirmishes and raids were frequent, and there were occasional pitched battles. Fortunately, the central mass of mountains acted as a kind of no man's land, a buffer zone between east and west. This made it difficult for either side to attack the other with a large army and win a decisive victory.

As an Irishman, Colum Cille can hardly have expected to be welcomed in Pictland. In spite of this, his mission to the Picts was remarkably successful. Saint Bede the Venerable, who wrote his famous *History of the English Church and People* around the year 730, tells us that Columba (Colum Cille) arrived among the Picts in the ninth year of the reign of their powerful King Brude, and that he converted them to the Christian faith by his word and example. Bede gives no further information about how this was accomplished so quickly and in the face of so many obstacles.

Adomnán fills in some of the gaps, though not as fully as we might wish. He is more concerned with the miracles Colum Cille is supposed to have worked among the Picts than with the practical work of evangelisation. He says little or nothing about the preaching and teaching and baptising, the organisation of Christian communities and the building of churches. He does not tell us how often Colum Cille went to Pictland or how long he spent there. Nonetheless, he provides us with some colourful incidents which help to fill in the background to the conversion of the Pictish people to the faith.

Colum Cille chose the obvious route on his journey to Pictland. Glen More, the Great Valley, runs straight as an arrow through the mountains from south-west to north-east. It could be traversed on foot or more comfortably by boat, using the long series of lakes, culminating in Loch Ness, which filled the bed of the valley and provided an almost continuous link between the North Sea and the Atlantic Ocean. At the River Ness, which joins Loch Ness to the sea, the saint and the monks who accompanied him had a memorable experience. Adomnán's description is so graphic that it has the feel of an eye-witness account.

> On another occasion, when the saint was spending some days in Pictland, he had to cross the River Ness. Arriving at the river bank, he saw some of the local people burying an unfortunate man. The grave-diggers told him that a short time earlier the man had been swimming in the river when a monster from the deep seized him in its mouth and savaged him horribly. Some men in a boat, too late to save his life, had succeeded in recovering his body by means of hooks.
>
> On hearing this, the holy man ordered one of his companions to swim across the river and bring back a boat which was moored to the opposite bank. In

response to the saint's command, Lugneus Mocumin immediately stripped off everything except his tunic and dived into the water. But the monster, whose hunger was not satisfied but rather sharpened by its previous victim, was lurking in the depths of the river. Sensing that the waters were being disturbed by a swimmer, it suddenly emerged and made for the man, with resounding roar and gaping jaws.

The blessed saint, seeing that everyone else, monks and natives alike, were frozen with terror, raised his holy hand and made the sign of the cross in the air. Then, invoking the name of God, he gave this command to the fierce beast, 'You will go no further. You will not touch this man. Turn and go at once.' At the sound of the saint's voice, the beast turned in terror and fled so quickly that it seemed to be pulled by ropes, though a few moments earlier it had been no more than the length of a short pole from Lugneus.

When the monks saw the beast vanishing and their fellow-soldier Lugneus coming back, safe and sound, in the boat, they were filled with wonder and praised God in his holy saint. Even the pagan natives were so overcome by the sight of this great miracle that they gave glory to the God of the Christians.

This is the first and possibly the only documented account of the Loch Ness monster. Too much credit should not, however, be attached to it. Sea and lake monsters occur frequently in the stories told about Colum Cille, and at least some of them must be inventions. The purpose of this narrative is not so much to tell us about the monster as to illustrate how Colum Cille's personality and sanctity and, above all, his power to work miracles impressed the Pictish people and opened their hearts to receive the message of the Gospel.

Less spectacular but no doubt more typical is another story from this period. 'During that time,' Adomnán begins, 'when Columba was spending some days in Pictland, a certain man and his family heard the saint proclaiming the word of life through an interpreter. Hearing he believed, believing he was baptised, he and his wife and his children and his whole household.' Adomnán goes on to describe how the man's son fell seriously ill and the pagan druids mocked the father and the Christian God who had no power to save his boy. Colum Cille arrived at the house and found the boy dead. He knelt in prayer beside him and prayed that he would be restored to life. His prayer was answered, the boy was restored to his parents and the heathen druids were confounded.

What is particularly interesting about this story is the brief light it throws on Colum Cille's missionary methods. He addressed crowds wherever he found them, men, women and children, probably in public places such as markets and harbours and fords. Unlike some other saints, he had no miraculous gift of tongues. In his preaching to the Picts he had to rely on interpreters. But even when filtered through another voice, his words could touch hearts and move minds. The man in the story heard and believed and was baptised before the raising of his son. It was not the saint's miracles that converted him but his words and his example.

On top of a steep hill overlooking the River Ness was the fortress of King Brude, the ruler of the Picts. He was a distant and somewhat sinister figure, a man who ruled with a rod of iron, before whom friends trembled as well as enemies. It was clear to Colum Cille that sooner or later he must confront the king. If he won the king's approval, the work of evangelisation would proceed more quickly and more smoothly.

As a man who had mixed with kings all his life, Colum Cille had no hesitation about making an uninvited visit to the royal residence. Adomnán describes the encounter between the two men with obvious enjoyment.

> The occasion came when the saint for the first time made the tiring journey to visit King Brude. As it happened, the king was so puffed up with royal pride that he arrogantly refused to have the gates of his fortress opened for the saint on his first visit. The man of God saw this when he and his companions arrived at the gateway, and at once he made the sign of the Lord's cross and struck the doors with his hand. The bolts shot back violently and the gates burst open of their own accord. The saint and his companions then entered through the open gateway.
>
> At the sight of this, the king and his council were struck with fear. They came out of the house and went to meet the holy man with every sign of respect, addressing him humbly and apologetically. From that day until the end of his life, the king honoured the holy and venerable man with the reverence which was his due.

Adomnán does not tell us whether the king became a Christian or not, but it is clear that he gave Colum Cille his full support and approval and thereby opened the way for the conversion of the Picts. The same could not be said of the druids and sorcerers and wizards who were part of the royal household and who saw their position threatened by the new religion. One of them, Briochan by name, was the king's foster-father, a man of great influence in the court and the possessor of strange occult powers. He opposed Colum Cille up to the bitter end, until the very last day of the saint's ministry in the country of the Picts.

Colum Cille was growing old and infirm and he decided that the time had come for him to return to his beloved Iona, the place where he wished to die. The faith had been proclaimed to the Picts and the Church had been firmly established in their country. There were many younger monks carrying on the work, men like Fintan, who was healed of a serious illness by the saint in Pictland and who went on to found a monastery in later life. Iona itself was a powerhouse of spiritual strength, from which missionaries would fan out across the whole of Scotland and then into the north of England. It was time for him to go home.

The news of the saint's departure spread rapidly and came to Briochan's ears. 'Tell me, Columba, when do you intend to sail?' he asked. 'We are starting our journey in three days' time, God willing and life permitting', said the saint. Briochan became aggressive. 'You won't do it. I have the power to summon up a contrary wind and to call down a dense fog upon you.' It was to be the final test of strength between the Christian God and the gods of the Picts.

On the day appointed, Colum Cille made his way to the place where a sailing-boat was ready to receive him. It was at the head of Loch Ness, where the lake flowed into the River Ness. A large crowd of people followed him, paying their last respects to their beloved saint. As they approached the lakeside, a strong wind began to blow in the opposite direction and a thick mist descended on the waters, blotting out all visibility. The druids and sorcerers were beside themselves with joy, congratulating one another on what looked like a total victory over Colum Cille and the new religion.

The saint was unperturbed. He boarded the boat and ordered the crew to hoist the sail and cast off. To the astonishment of all present, the boat started to do the impossible, moving forward effortlessly in the teeth of the gale. As the boat continued on its way, the wind dropped and then changed direction, propelling the boat gently to its destination. 'Let the reader reflect,' writes Adomnán, 'on the greatness and goodness of this holy man, in whom almighty God chose to glorify his name by working such mighty miracles before the eyes of a pagan crowd.'

The Company of Angels

The closing years of Colum Cille's life were a time of peace and serenity. He lived until his mid-seventies, an unusually advanced age in those days. He remained strong in will and clear in mind, ruling the monastery firmly but gently, in constant demand from visitors and pilgrims. He spent much of his time in the company of angels, who were as real and as present to him as the monks who formed his growing community. He was aware too of the presence of evil, personified in the demons that he saw waiting to claim the souls of those who died at enmity with God. His gifts of clairvoyance and his powers of prophecy became more remarkable than ever. One day he had a vision of the monastery he had founded at Durrow in Ireland, and he saw a monk falling from the roof of the great house which was being built there. He called on the angels for help and one of them caught the monk in his arms before he touched the ground.

It may have been during this period that he wrote his great Latin hymn *Altus Prosator*. This long and powerful statement of the Christian faith begins with the Most High Father (*Altus Prosator*) creating the universe and ends with the righteous entering into Heaven to live in eternal glory. The stanza describing the Day of Judgment has been memorably translated into English by Helen Waddell.

> Day of the king most righteous
>   The day is nigh at hand;
> The day of wrath and vengeance,
>   And darkness on the land.

Day of thick clouds and voices,
    Of mighty thundering,
A day of narrow anguish
    And bitter sorrowing.
The love of women's over,
    And ended is desire,
Men's strife with men is quiet,
    And the world lusts no more.

He himself was living increasingly in another world. Stories multiplied about the light that seemed to surround him during his times of prayer. Once, when he was visiting his monastery on the Isle of Hinba, the Holy Spirit took possession of him for three whole days. He remained in his hut for all that time, neither eating nor drinking, cut off from the world. Those outside could hear him singing strange chants and after dark could see light of an unnatural brilliance escaping through the keyholes and chinks in the doors. All he would say afterwards was that he had been given knowledge of many secrets and a new understanding of the scriptures.

The more favours he was granted, the more he tried to conceal them. A young monk was praying one night in a side chapel of the church on Iona. Colum Cille came in and started to pray, unaware of the young man's presence. At once, a light brighter than the sun filled the church and the monk had to cover his eyes for protection. Then the saint left and the light died away.

The next day the saint sent for the monk and said, 'Last night you did well in the sight of God, by casting down your eyes for fear of his brilliance. Had you not done so, your eyes might have been blinded by the overwhelming radiance. But you must take care to do this: you must tell no-one about this vision of light as long as I am alive.' His reason for concealing this and other similar incidents was to avoid crowds of wonder-seekers flocking to Iona and disrupting the daily work and prayer of himself and his community. But nothing he said or did could prevent his fame from spreading. By the time of his death, he was the spiritual leader and his monastery the spiritual centre of the whole of Scotland.

Adomnán finishes his book with his famous account of the last days of Colum Cille. In this he abandons all the elaborate structures and categories and stylistic flourishes that make many of the earlier pages seem artificial and overwrought. Simple, direct, totally credible and obviously based closely on the testimony of eye-witnesses, it is a small masterpiece of hagiography.

Colum Cille thought it likely that he would die in 593, the thirtieth anniversary of the founding of the monastery in Iona. One day that year he was filled with joy when he had a vision of angels coming to receive his soul into Heaven. But they hesitated and then turned back, recalled by the prayers of the many churches who could not bear to lose him. He was consoled when he was told that in another four years he would be taken for sure and that his passing would be sudden and without pain.

The prophecy was fulfilled in the summer of 597. One day towards the end of May, the saint, no longer able to walk any distance, had himself brought in a cart to where the monks were working on the west side of the island. 'In April, last month at Easter time,' he told them, 'I was filled with a desire to be taken to Christ the Lord, which he would have granted if I had asked. But so as not to turn the joy of the festival into sorrow, I preferred to postpone for a little while the day of my departure from the world.' The monks were devastated by his words, but he comforted them and blessed the whole island before being brought home again.

At Mass on the following Sunday, they noticed him looking up and smiling with joy. He explained afterwards that he had seen an angel in the church above the heads of the worshippers. God had sent his messenger to reclaim a loan that was very dear to him and to bless his people. Not until later did they realise that the loan was Colum Cille's soul, which was soon to be returned to its maker.

The week passed uneventfully until the following Saturday, 8 June. The saint and his faithful servant Diarmaid went to the barn to bless the grain stored there. Colum Cille said he was glad to see that there would be a plentiful supply of food for the monks after he had gone. Diarmaid remonstrated with him. 'Father,' he said, 'all this year you keep making us sad by talking so often about your passing.' The saint asked him to keep what he was about to say a secret. Then he told him that at midnight, the end of that very day, he would be taken to the Lord.

The two men made their way back to the monastery. On the way, the saint sat down and rested for a little while. Diarmaid was beside him, unable to control his tears. They saw coming towards them the faithful white horse which was used to bring milk from the cowshed to the monastery. The horse came right up to the saint and, laid its head against his chest. Its eyes began to fill with tears and it wept for the saint as if it was a human being. Diarmaid tried to drive it away but the saint said, 'Let it be. Because of its love for me it is shedding bitter tears on my breast. You are a man with a rational mind, but you would not have known of my departure if I had not told you. But the Creator has chosen to reveal to this dumb and mindless animal that its master is going away.' Then he blessed the horse as it moved off sorrowfully.

The saint stood up and continued homewards. He paused on a small mound overlooking the monastery and raised his hands in blessing. He spoke of the greatness in store for this humble place and of the kings and saints who would come to pay it homage. Then he reached his hut, went in and calmly resumed work on the book which he had been copying. It was the Book of Psalms. He wrote for some time until he had finished the tenth verse of Psalm 33 which ends with the words: 'Those who seek the Lord shall not lack anything that is good.' Then he laid down his pen for ever, saying, 'Let Baithene write what follows.' Baithene was the monk who was to succeed him as abbot.

The saint went as usual to the church for vespers, the evening prayer of the monks. When it was over he came back to his room and lay down on his bed, which was made of rock with a stone for a pillow. Resting peacefully, he gave his last instructions to the brethren. Diarmaid alone was there to hear and remember what he said. 'My children, these are my last words to you. You must love one other truly and in peace. If you do this in accordance with the example of the holy fathers, then God, who gives strength to the good, will come to your aid; and I, dwelling in his presence, will intercede on your behalf. And you will be given a generous portion not only of the goods needed for this life, but of the eternal rewards prepared for those who observe the law of God.'

He remained there in quiet contentment until he heard the sound of the bell, calling the community to the church for the midnight office. It was the summons he was waiting for. He leapt up and, despite his age and infirmity, ran all the way to the church. He arrived there before the others, went in and knelt in front of the altar. Diarmaid, hurrying behind, saw the church suddenly fill with light. It faded again as the other monks arrived, leaving the place in total darkness, 'Where are you, Father?' Diarmaid cried as he groped his way to where the saint was lying. He raised him up a little from the floor and cradled his head in his arms. The other monks brought lights and stood around him. His eyes were shining with joy, as he saw the angels coming to meet him. He tried to bless the monks but he could neither speak nor move his hand. Seeing this, Diarmaid lifted the saint's right hand and moved it in blessing over the monks. The saint tried to move his hand in unison with Diarmaid, the strength of his will overcoming for a moment the weakness of his body. Then his hand fell and the light faded from his eyes. He was dead. It was Sunday, 9 June 597.

More than a hundred miles away some men were fishing in the River Finn in Donegal. Among them was a monk from one of Colum Cille's monasteries. To their astonishment the night sky suddenly became as bright as day. They looked to the east and saw what looked like a huge column of fire reaching from earth to heaven. After a time it faded and night returned, leaving the men filled with wonder and apprehension. Next day they found that many other fishermen had seen the same marvel. Years later the monk met the young Adomnán and gave him his eye-witness testimony. It was only one of many strange phenomena that marked the passing of one of Ireland's greatest saints.

On Iona the monks were mourning their loss and preparing for three days of prayer and solemn ritual. A young monk had once told Colum Cille that people would come from every direction and fill the island for his funeral. The saint told him he was mistaken. His funeral would be attended only by the members of his own monastic family, the Iona community. It happened as he foretold. For the three days of his obsequies, a howling gale cut off all access to the island. His body was clothed in white linen and buried in a humble grave to the chanting of the monks. As soon as the grave was filled, the wind dropped and people could come to pray at his burial place. They came in their hundreds and in their thousands and it became the most hallowed graveyard in Scotland. For many centuries the Scottish kings were to be brought there for burial.

Ireland bore him, Scotland holds his remains. Each country has precious memories of his work and witness. The Irish remember the young firebrand who set his country aflame with his zeal and covered half the land with monasteries and churches. They know his faults and they forgive them. He was a human saint. If his fiery temper led him to do wrong, he made magnificent amends. The Scots have gentler memories of a gentler man, the father of Christianity in their country. Others had come before him, preached their message and built their churches. Their message had been forgotten and their churches had fallen into ruin. But Colum Cille built on a firmer foundation, the rock-like solidity of his faith, and what he built remains to this day.

His influence goes far beyond Ireland and Scotland. After his death, monks from Iona continued his work. The most famous of them, the great St Aidan, brought Christianity to the kingdoms of the north of England. But it was not only the community in Iona that kept their founder's spirit alive. All over Ireland, young men were inspired by his example. They pledged themselves to leave their homeland for ever and devote themselves to the preaching of the Gospel. He was still alive when his near namesake, St Columbanus, sailed from Bangor with twelve companions and rocked barbarian Europe to its roots. Ireland was no longer an inward-looking country, content to keep the faith to itself. The long list of Irish saints whose names are commemorated throughout the central and western countries of Europe bears witness to the way in which Ireland repaid its debt. The faith and culture and civilisation which had been almost extinguished by the barbarians were preserved in Ireland and brought back by its monks and missionaries. It was a turning-point in the history of civilisation and it was Colum Cille who led the way.